LONELINESS BREAKTHROUGH BLUEPRINT

LONELINESS BREAKTHROUGH BLUEPRINT

Strategies for Unlocking Paths to Belonging

INNER POWER

Inner Strength Counselling

CONTENTS

CHAPTER 1

A Personal Journey

Loneliness is something I intimately understand. If you're here and feeling the weight of isolation, I want you to know that you're not alone. The motivation behind creating this book stems from my own experiences. I've delved into those hollow, empty emotions multiple times, knowing intimately the grip of loneliness.

I've felt its suffocating grasp – the endless, dragging hours that feel like days, the desolate nights where tears soak my pillow in silence, the urge to escape the next day, and even the haunting thoughts of ending it all.

It's an emotion that doesn't discriminate. Whether you have a significant other or not, there are parts of your loneliness that others simply cannot grasp. Even after pouring your heart out to friends, family, or professionals, that sense of understanding seems elusive. You want them to feel your pain, yet it feels impossible.

But here's the good news for all of us feeling the pangs of loneliness: I've weathered through it, and I've discovered ways to overcome if not entirely alleviate, the pain.

In this book, my aim is to achieve a few crucial things:

- Grasping the theory behind loneliness to gain a deeper understanding of yourself.
- Recognizing and processing the emotions tied to loneliness.
- Cultivating a healthy sense of self-love to combat these challenges.
- Offering practical steps to break free from the cycle of loneliness.
- Replacing feelings of isolation with positive, healthy thoughts.

It's my sincerest hope that once you've journeyed through these pages, you'll be better equipped to manage loneliness. Even if you're not feeling lonely, perhaps you know someone who is. Use the insights here to brighten their world and make it a better place.

CHAPTER 2

Understanding and Overcoming the Grasp of Loneliness

At some point in life, everyone encounters the emotion of loneliness. In today's rapidly advancing technological era, this feeling seems to be on a swift incline.

Loneliness is more than just a mere absence of company; it's an emotional state. It encapsulates a profound sense of disconnection from those around us, plunging individuals into a deep void where the presence of others seems devoid of meaning.

It's crucial to differentiate loneliness from being alone.

Solitude doesn't always equate to loneliness. There are instances when solitude can be rejuvenating, offering moments for self-reflection and rediscovery.

Identifying the Telltale Signs

Are you experiencing the symptoms of loneliness as you read this? Let's explore some common indicators:

- Feeling that your problems are too unique for others to understand.
- Believing that everyone else has friends while you do not.
- Experiencing extreme self-consciousness in your actions.
- Getting excessively embarrassed over mistakes.
- Feeling suffocated by the noise of crowds.
- Sensing disconnection despite being amongst others.
- Battling shyness and fear around people.
- Encountering low self-esteem.
- Reacting with anger, defensiveness, and criticism, even when it's not directed at you.
- Avoiding interactions with strangers out of fear.
- Convinced that something is inherently wrong with you.
- Suffering from anxiety and sadness, convinced of your isolation.
- Losing assertiveness, feeling "invisible."
- Resisting change and new experiences.
- Contemplating suicide, feeling that nothing else matters.

Understanding these signs is a crucial step toward addressing and overcoming the grip of loneliness.

CHAPTER 3

Surrounded but Alone

Have you ever felt the frustrating gap of misunderstanding with your spouse or partner, despite their physical presence? Surrounded by people, yet still feeling engulfed by loneliness?

This feeling arises because each of us is inherently unique. No one in the vast expanse of the universe possesses the exact blend of personality, ideas, lifestyle, and needs that you do – not even identical twins. How can anyone possibly fulfill all these diverse needs?

Consider this biblical quote: "Why worry about a speck in your friend's eye when you have a log in your own?" This adage teaches us a crucial lesson. Understanding that others aren't obligated to meet all our needs helps in curbing expectations, leading to less disappointment and judgment.

By embracing this wisdom, we begin to expect less from others, easing the pain of unmet expectations and fostering acceptance. It's the first step toward alleviating loneliness – granting others some leeway.

Remember, we are greatly influenced by the company we keep. If you're constantly surrounded by negativity, it's no wonder that you might feel lonely and downtrodden. Just as children distance themselves from negative parents or certain friend groups, don't let toxic influences drain your energy.

Being mindful of the impact of the people we surround ourselves with is key. It's essential to gravitate towards positive, supportive circles that uplift and empower, contributing to a more fulfilling life.

CHAPTER 4

The Human Connection Struggle

Loneliness, a universal agony, touches the hearts of people worldwide, regardless of their stature. Even iconic figures admired by millions, like Janis Joplin and Kurt Cobain, have grappled with unfulfillment.

This feeling often stems from our inability to express love toward others. The symptoms of loneliness amplify the pain, redirecting our focus inward, resulting in self-preoccupation that obstructs our ability to connect with others.

Consider a moment when you've had a stomachache. Who occupied your thoughts at that moment? It highlights our inclination toward self-absorption, painting a world deeply entrenched in pain and self-focus.

Moreover, this pain isn't fleeting like a stomachache. What was once dubbed a mid-life crisis now seems to afflict younger generations, leading to a surge in suicide rates and psychiatric conditions plaguing our world today.

The foundation of trust among people is crumbling, with fewer individuals willing to open up. Failing to be open ourselves triggers the symptoms of loneliness, making it challenging for others to open up to us.

As the adage goes, to have friends, one must first be a friend. Initiating openness and friendship is key to combatting the isolating grip of loneliness.

CHAPTER 5

To Love

The absence of love nurtures the seeds of loneliness within a person's heart. It's a chilling reality that our identities are significantly shaped by others – a concept reflected in the notion that we are a composite of the five people we spend the most time with.

Who we are today is, in part, a reflection of those who have embraced us with love or those who have chosen not to.

Love, a life-giving force, begins with self-love. It's crucial to acknowledge that in order to effectively love others, we must first nurture love within ourselves. After all, you can't give what you don't possess!

Feeling infatuated with a beautiful person or admiring someone's attractiveness might not be genuine love if self-love is absent. The sentiment of being incomplete without someone else may not necessarily be love either.

Admiration, worship, or even sacrificing for someone out of a selfish ego-driven motive doesn't necessarily constitute love.

Love is an action—a verb. It transcends feelings and manifests through deliberate actions. Loving oneself lays the groundwork for loving others authentically. Without this foundation, displays of affection may be hollow, merely deceptive acts.

But how do we learn to love ourselves, especially if we've never experienced love? Exploring this very question will be the focus of the upcoming chapter.

CHAPTER 6

The Paradox of Love

The first step in combating loneliness is learning to love, but the paradox of love is complex and demands examination.

In the depths of loneliness, we feel trapped within an unbearable confinement—a self-focused state akin to a persistent stomach ache. Seeking to fill this emptiness, we often chase after others, hoping for their love to alleviate our loneliness.

In this pursuit, we might engage in favor-trading or actions to win affection, mistakenly believing that the love we crave can only come from others.

Yet, here lies the paradox of love:

Seeking to fill our own loneliness through external love leads us only to deeper despair. The more we chase after the love we lack, the more elusive it becomes. When our focus remains fixed on fulfilling our own needs, our capacity to love diminishes.

The solution lies in shifting our focus away from ourselves towards others. Embracing a mindset of giving love unconditionally, without expecting anything in return, renders us more lovable and eventually draws love from others.

Our ability to love is inherent in us all. It's the degree to which we selflessly give that determines the love we receive in return.

Choosing to love without attachment to personal gain is akin to a selfless donation, not a transaction. When we ask, "What have you done for me?" in return for our affection, we fail to embody genuine love.

Even if initially our capacity to love is limited, the love we give will enable growth, resulting in greater reciprocated affection. However, the essence of this selfless giving demands our focus to always remain outward, away from self-concern, for it to truly flourish.

CHAPTER 7

Mindset Matters

The phrase "As a man thinks, so is he" holds profound truth in how we perceive and present ourselves.

Have you ever noticed the subtle differences in how people address each other? Some receive respectful greetings like "Good Morning, Sir," while others get more casual acknowledgments like "Hey Bud" or "Hey, Mac."

The way others react to us often mirrors our self-perception. People tend to judge based on appearances or attire, but more significantly, the way we think about ourselves reflects outwardly. It's an unfair yet evident truth that our inner thoughts manifest in our outward presentation and life experiences.

The Law of Attraction isn't novel; it's a reflection of reality. It aligns with Murphy's Law—unwanted outcomes tend to occur frequently. Remember the dropped buttered toast landing butter side down? It's just one manifestation of this phenomenon.

Reflect on past experiences. In school, did you ever silently hope not to be called upon when unsure of an answer? Yet, somehow, the teacher seemed to pick you out of the crowd. It's almost as if they could read your thoughts and gauge your level of preparedness.

So, how does this relate to overcoming loneliness?

If you emit an aura of feeling unwanted or unloved, it unconsciously repels others, reinforcing feelings of rejection. Instead of projecting an image of an unwanted puppy, change your internal narrative.

Repeatedly affirm to yourself, "I am attractive, lovable, and great company." While it may be challenging to genuinely convince ourselves of these traits, the practice of positive affirmation tricks our minds into believing it. We may not control others' perceptions, but this self-affirmation influences our mindset.

Give it a try and witness the subtle yet significant changes it brings!

CHAPTER 8

Strategies to Conquer Loneliness

Addressing loneliness requires proactive measures aimed at fostering connections, nurturing self-worth, and cultivating meaningful relationships. Here are practical strategies to achieve this:

1. **Reaffirmation:**
   - Remind yourself that loneliness is transient and will gradually wane over time.
2. **Initiating Dialogue:**
   - Challenge yourself to engage with new individuals; the initial step is often the most daunting yet pivotal for momentum.
3. **Exploring Novel Activities:**
   - Participate in activities aligning with your genuine

interests, providing opportunities to meet like-minded individuals.

4. **Joining Social Groups:**
   - Engage in church groups, organizations, or clubs that resonate with your passions to expand your social network.

5. **Avoiding Solitary Triggers:**
   - Limit exposure to melancholic music or media reinforcing feelings of seclusion.

6. **Embracing Openness:**
   - Approach others without preconceived judgments from past encounters.

7. **Progressive Friendship Building:**
   - Foster friendships gradually, allowing for a natural evolution in sharing personal emotions.

8. **Valuing Diverse Relationships:**
   - Recognize the potential for satisfaction in both platonic and casual relationships.

9. **Holistic Well-being:**
   - Maintain a balanced life through proper nutrition, exercise, and sufficient sleep to mitigate depression.

10. **Reflection and Introspection:**
    - Embrace solitude for introspection and self-examination.

11. **Balanced Support Seeking:**
    - Avoid excessively burdening friends with personal issues; maintain a healthy exchange instead of constant reliance.

12. **Gratitude and Positive Memories:**
    - Reflect on positive memories and count your blessings to uplift your spirits.

13. **Skill Enhancement:**
    - Acquire new skills or achieve personal goals to bolster self-confidence.

14. **Professional Assistance:**
    - Consider seeking medical advice for persistent depression; medication can address chemical imbalances contributing to loneliness.

15. **Counseling and Spiritual Support:**
    - Seek counseling for private discussions and find solace in prayer for mental peace and spiritual guidance.

Incorporating these strategies into your life can empower you to proactively combat loneliness, fostering a more enriching social and emotional existence.

CHAPTER 9

Beware the Lonely Hero

Amidst the battle against loneliness, a word of caution emerges:

Beware of assuming a heroic stance solely because of loneliness. Surprisingly, self-pity is a subtle manifestation of pride. While the proud boast of accomplishments, those in self-pity take pride in their suffering.

Dwelling excessively in loneliness is perilous; it contradicts our innate human need for connections and relationships. This inherent aspect of human nature remains ingrained, evident even in hypothetical scenarios of solitary jungle existence involving interactions with animals or plants.

Prolonged loneliness can lead to worrisome outcomes:

- Loneliness Addiction: The individual rejects attempts to reconnect, causing anguish to those trying to help.
- Deteriorating Relationships: Surrounding relationships may crumble, leading the lonely individual to feel justified in their belief that others never cared.
- Embracing Loneliness: Immunity to the pain of loneliness sets in, making it a comfortable yet detrimental way of life, leading to reluctance to seek change.

The influence of this loneliness can spread, affecting others similarly afflicted.

Let this serve as a compelling motivation for action. Act now, rather than waiting.

CHAPTER 10

The Interconnectedness of Life

Amidst our pursuits for wealth, fame, and power, a story unfolds to reveal the true essence of life's meaning.

Consider the Colorado aspen tree—found not in solitary existence but in clusters, forming groves. These trees interconnect through their roots, sending up new shoots that bind them together in a network of mutual support.

Similarly, the towering California redwoods, despite their immense height, possess shallow roots that stretch wide to capture surface water. These roots intertwine with neighboring redwoods, creating a strong interlocked system.

In the face of adversity, these trees stand firm because they are not isolated; they lean on each other for support. Much like them, humans are deeply connected by the roots of family and friendship. Our survival and well-being are intertwined with our relationships.

Just as the aspen and redwood trees support each other against storms, we, too, need the support of others in the tempests of life. Our capacity to thrive and endure adversity is bolstered by the connections we forge and nurture with others.

Have you been navigating this journey on your own? Consider the possibility that it's time to allow someone else to provide support or lend a hand. Conversely, there might be someone who needs your support and strength to lean on.